The Reasons
Why They Are Rich
and You Are Not

By

T.D. Lowman

ISBN: 0-75965-506-5

This book is printed on acid free paper.

1stBooks – rev. 9/18/01

DEDICATIONS

I WANT TO THANK GOD

—FOR MAKING THIS ALL POSSIBLE

I WANT TO THANK MY MOTHER

—FOR INSPIRING ME AND

SHOWING ME LOVE ALL THE TIME

I WANT TO THANK MY FATHER

—FOR ALWAYS BEING A GREAT

FATHER; SHOWING ME

HOW TO BE A MAN

I WANT TO THANK MY BROTHERS

—FOR NEVER ALLOWING ANYONE

TO TAKE ADVANTAGE OF ME

I WANT TO THANK MY GRANDPARENTS

—FOR ALWAYS SHOWING

ME LOVE WHEN I THOUGHT

NO ONE CARED

I WANT TO THANK ALL MY FRIENDS

—YOU ALL HAVED HELPED

GROWING UP

I WANT TO THANK THE REST OF MY FAMILY

—SORRY I HAD TO KEEP THIS

PART SHORT BUT YOU WILL

NEVER BE FORGOTTEN

FOR THE PEOPLE WHO DON'T LIKE ME

—I JUST WANT TO SAY THANK

YOU; YOU MAY HAVE PUSHED ME

MORE THAN ANYONE ELSE

I JUST WANT TO SAY I LOVE YOU

LOOK FOR THE SUMMER OF 2002
I WILL BE WRITING A BOOK CALLED
"SO WHAT ARE WE AFRAID OF?"

CONTENTS

HAVING A VISION

Having a vision is very important. You can say it may be the most important thing. Most rich people have a very clear vision. Here are a few things they envision before any action takes place: some of the places they want to go; what type of car they want to drive; the time they want to spend with their family; the type of house they want to live in. I remember the first time I wanted to buy a house. I was very happy and excited. The reason I was happy and excited was because I had a vision of the way I wanted the house to look. I wanted each floor to have a different look to it. It was a must that I envisioned all of these things before it took place. Well, the house I was interested in was a foreclosed property. For those of you who may not know what that means, it is a house someone may have had in the past but lost for whatever reason to the city or to a bank.

The reason they did lose the house I never found out. This house needed all the help it could get. The porch was falling apart, most of the windows were wrecked and pipes were taken from out of the walls. There were holes in the floor. I can say it needed at least $60,000 worth of work, but I did not care because I knew I had a vision. My friends and family called me crazy. I was dating a female, and she thought I was crazy. Even the real-estate agent and mortgage loan officer did not even think it was a good idea. He even tried to talk me out of it a few times. Everyone thought I was crazy, everyone except for me. I did not care what they said. I would not change my mind, but that was because I had a vision. So I ended up purchasing the house anyway. The closing date came and I went and bought the house. The next move was getting the contractors to start working on the house.

Days and weeks passed until the contractors started working on my new house. After a while the house started to look better and better. My parents started to change their minds, as well as everyone else who thought it was a bad idea for me to purchase this house. To be quite honest, the house ended up coming out better than what I envisioned. See, this is something that can happen to you if you focus on your vision. When the house was done, it was beautiful. The house looked like a palace from outside. The rooms had all new windows. I got brand new carpets put on the floors. The porch was done all over with a very nice shine. The basement was done all over. The kitchen and bathroom looked the way most bathrooms look in a five-star hotel. The house was terrific. To be honest, the house came out to be better than I had imagined.

See, when you have a vision you are not worried about the way things look at that present time. You are not worried about what others may feel about what you are trying to do. One of the many reasons rich people don't care what some people may say is because they see a bigger picture than what the world may see. You know the way things might be physically, it will not stay the same. You know deep down inside those things will end up being the way you envision it.

Having a vision is always the first step to anything. Right now I want you to picture your goals in life. Take 5–10 minutes every day to picture yourself doing something you always wanted to do. As the days go by, I want you to dream a little more and more. Just like some rich people. My main goal was to be a motivational speaker. This vision came to me in a dream I once had. I always wanted to help people out who really needed help but I never knew how.

Every day passed and I would think of every way in the world to help someone out who needed some type of help, some type of direction. I will tell you how my goal came to me in my dream. For two weeks straight my car had broken down and I was sick with the flu. So most of the time I was taking medicine that made me very drowsy. So I was asleep very often. What happened then was every day I would have different types of dream. First I dreamed of myself in some big ballroom like in a hotel, sitting in the back of the room every day. I always pictured myself helping people reach their goals in life, but I never could put it all together. Every time I dreamed, more and more features would be added to what I was seeing in my dream.

The next couple of days I would see the people seated next to me. I could see that it was breakfast food being served. I felt I had something to do with it because I enjoyed eating In the morning. On top of that, they were serving my favorite foods. I know I was involved somehow or some way. Day by day would go by but I still had not seen who was at the front of this room hosting this presentation. During the whole presentation I heard a lot of different voices coming from the audience.

One of the problems I was having was I still could not hear the voice of the host. However, I could tell by the reaction of the people in the audience that this person was saying something to really get to their souls, because some people were shedding tears and some were shaking their heads as if they felt very motivated or like they felt encouraged. But I could not hear what was being said. I could not even hear what the subject was based on. All I knew was, I was there seated in the back, very confused, not knowing what in the world was going on. Till one day I saw the front of the room. In the front of the room I saw all my friends. That made me very confused. I kept asking myself, well, why would my friends be there in the front but not with me? At this point I was going crazy because I thought it was a dream about me being dead or about them being successful. So I figured that I was someone just to see them. I felt they moved on with their lives and forgot about me, but boy, was I wrong. See, my friends and I always talked about making a grand entrance, going somewhere if we were to become rich and famous, no matter what the event would be—concert, party, or any other big event. But that was only if we ever made it in life. Well, that is exactly what I was doing in my dream. I had made it, not to brag about what I had, but to tell the world forget what the world will tell you. You can make it, just believe in yourself and you can do it. See, in the dream one of my friends became a motivational speaker as well.

I was a guest speaker, pretending to be in the audience. So I woke up in shock, not because I was a motivational speaker, not because the way I handled everything and I loved it. It was the way I picked up the microphone and started talking to everyone like I had been speaking for years.

I was amazed not because I was sitting in the audience, not because I saw my friends supporting me all the way, not because of the way I handled the crowd, but the way I carried myself, the way I was dressed. The way I was in control of everything. I fell in love with the attitude that I saw myself having. It was the energy that I had during the show and after. When I woke up that morning, I sat up for a while and just thought to myself. After a while I felt a tear in my eyes, not because I am emotional, not because I had butterflies in my stomach, but because I woke up and said this is it, this is what I have been looking for all these years. I just loved the idea of me helping everyone that I can. I wanted to be the person to put the faith into people to strive for their goals. The dream I had that morning became the turning point in my life. It was no more guessing what I wanted to do. My decision was already made for me.

Most people see things the way they are and that is that. They don't see their situation getting better. They don't think things can change. They figure it is this way because this is the way it is supposed to be. The whole thing is, you have got to feel it can change. You have to know things can get better. Most people just can't envision good things in their heads. To be honest, if you are like that, it is not your fault. It may be the way you were raised, or it could be negative things that always happened so you tend to think negative all the time.

From this point on you must tell yourself, everything is going to change. You have to feel it. Carry a new attitude with you. Stop having that losing spirit with you. You have to develop a winning attitude. Tell yourself you are a survivor, tell yourself you can beat whatever it is in life that is stopping you. Once you envision things getting better (and things can get better), you must try a little harder. Rich people give everything their best, no matter what it is. They always have that survivor mentality. They give it a try and maybe whatever they envision may not work for them. So what? I guarantee you they will end up finding something else they would love to do.

Try to become very good at whatever it is you are doing. No matter what your vision is, you must stick with it. But on top of that, your vision must be put together by some type of plan. To write down a plan is very important.

WRITING OUT A PLAN

Having a plan is very important. Everything in life that is done well must have some type of plan. It is important for you to sit down and really think about what it is you want to do. Rich people always have some type of game plan together. Even if their first one looks like it is not going to work, they always have a backup plan. If you are reading this book and you are not sure what you want to do, that is fine. Do not panic. I want you to take a second to write down a few things. First write down five things that you like.

I don't care what it is. It can be just driving around, it can be just planting flowers in the yard. It can be shopping, surfing on the Net. No matter what it is, write it down. If you have more than five or ten things, that is even better. Then write down five things you like a lot and then write down five things you love. After that, you write down at least ten things you would not mind getting paid for. Let me explain something to you right now: if you wrote something down at least two or three times, I am convinced that whatever it may be, you should be doing that with your life. There are so many different things that can be done in this day and age. Within these items, circle the ones you really enjoyed doing and would like to do them again. The more you circle, the better for you.

You have just found something that can make you rich. Forget about what it is you have to do to get there, forget about how old you are, forget about what has happened to someone else who tried it, because that person is not you. You can do it! Now you start writing down some dates to go along with your goals, and there it is: you have made a plan. Now, it is not a must to write down an actual date. You may just write down some type of timeframe, such as a week or a month. If you really want to play it safe, you will.

If your plan is to become a doctor, you should know you have to go to college, then after that medical school. Forget about how many years you are going to be in school. It will all pay off when you are done with school. If this is going to be your dream, make it happen. I don't know your situation, but if you are doing something that you do not enjoy doing, or worse, something you hate doing, you must ask yourself why? After you ask yourself why, then you must write down the things you like, love and enjoy. Because if you are doing something that you hate and you continue to, you will start hating everything in your life. It is a good chance you might start hating yourself.

The harsh reality of it all is if you don't have a plan for this world, it will have a plan for you. You have to see the pattern. You go from newspaper to newspaper, or from website to website. Your next step is from interview to interview. Your next move is from check to check. That can be forever and ever until you stop working and the process starts all over again, unless you are going to retire. Think about it: was your plan when you were younger to live from check to check, to get a certain amount of sick days and vacation days? Most people who are rich do not have to live this way. They do not have to live from check to check and you don't either.

You must plan out what you want out of life. When it is all said and done, you want to be able to look back and look at all the stuff you have accomplished. But you must start off with a plan. If your plan is to go to college to be a doctor, which means after college you have to go to medical school, then that is your plan.

Forget about how many years you are going to be in school. Forget about having to give up stuff like hanging out. The reason is because you have a plan. You must stick to your plan. You will find where your plans can seem real rough. You must stick to your plan. See once someone rich writes out their plan, they follow their dreams. After that they stop chasing. Once you chase your dreams, your dream will chase you. That happens all the time. No matter what your dream is. Once you chase it, your dream will soon chase you.

You may be tired of the way people treat you, talk to you. Well, it is time to change that. Forget the world, say the world is yours. Change it, make the world work for you. How long are you going to allow these people to tell you what to do? Think about this: you get a certain amount of vacation days and sick days. Who in the world are they to say you are going to be able to be sick a certain amount of days? Who in an office can say yes, John has only 10 vacation days a year? Don't you deserve more? Just to take a vacation, what happens when they say no, I can't allow you to go on vacation? You are like their child. You might as well call them mommy or daddy. But all this comes from not having a plan. So sit down and write out a plan together. It is not that hard to put a plan together. All you have to do is just write down what it is you really want to do. After you write down what it is you want to do, try to put some dates to go along with that. In some cases you may just have to expect that if you write down a plan with a date, it can take longer. That is fine; as long as you reach your goal, it should not matter when you get there. As long as you write out a plan, everything will be alright. You have to be patient as well. Don't be too patient, because along with having patients and writing out a plan, you must take action, you will make it.

TAKING ACTION

Rich people take action better than anyone else. They are willing to do whatever it is they have to do to get to that next level. They don't talk about it. They *are* about it. They put their pride aside and forget all the excuses on why they can't do it or make it. It does not matter who it is, everyone famous has mastered something in life. I don't care if it is movie stars, athletes, entertainers or just salespeople who reach the million-dollar status. They all have mastered something.

Of course that all came from hard work taking action. Practice, practice and more practice. No one is perfect, but it may have been sometimes where someone rich had performed perfectly. That is from taking action. The only way you can succeed in life is when you take action. Having a vision is good, very good. Having a written plan is great. But if you don't take action, you are not going to get where you want to go. Being rich is going to take a while, depending on what it is you want to do. For some of you it may take months, for some it can take years. It also can be at least 25 years, but as long as you get there, who cares? As long as you become rich it does not matter. You just have to make sure you stick with it and stay very, very patient.

BEING PATIENT

Most rich people are very, very patient. They have to be patient to be able to make that first big break. Their patience leads up to their first big check. Being patient is as important as any other subject in this book. If you don't have patience, you may end up living life with a lot of regrets and frustration that will build up more and more as the years pass you by. You may be regretting something in your life right now. Don't think about it; let that go. There are a few things that most people have no patience with: school, work, family members, relationships, paychecks, working out (fitness), and the list goes on and on.

I remember a few years ago hearing this story about Carlos Perez. Carlos was about 25. He had just gotten married a few months earlier. Everything was going fine in Carlos's life, except he did not like working at the auto body shop. He hated going home with dirty hands, smelling like oil and always having to work. He worked that job till he felt he could not work there anymore. But the only thing was that he loved cars. His next job was working in the kitchen of a fancy restaurant. This restaurant was very huge. It was not a five-star restaurant, but it was very nice. He worked there for about four years but he started disliking what he was doing. Next he got a job at UPS. He worked there for about seven months, but this job was killing him. So he went two months without a job. He was very depressed, till one of his friends found him a manager job at a fast food restaurant. He was working there, he liked it all right, but he still loved looking at cars and he just still loved cars, period. The location of this fast food restaurant was on a highway. Right across the highway was a car dealership.

One day, one of the car salesmen came over to the store that Carlos was working at and ordered some food. While the car salesman was waiting for his food to be made, Carlos went over to him and asked if the salesman could help him get a new car. So like most car salesmen, he said, "Sure, I can get you a car. Just stop by after work and tell the receptionist to page Bobby to the showroom."

Well, then it was time for Carlos to get off work. He walked across the road to the car dealership. While Carlos was walking to the showroom, he saw the car he always wanted. While he was looking at the car, there was a couple coming out of the showroom. The look on their faces was as if they had given up on trying to get the car they wanted. So they started making remarks about the car and Carlos said, "This is a great car."

They said, "Really?"

He said, "Yes, this car has child safety locks," and he just started to name all the things that this car could offer to an owner.

While the couple was outside talking to Carlos, Bobby was inside telling the boss that he felt he lost this deal with the couple that was outside. The boss said, "Don't worry about it. Where is the guy you are supposed to meet today?"

Bobby looked outside and saw him talking to the couple. He thought that Carlos was ruining everything for him. But within two minutes, the couple came back and said they wanted to buy the car. Bobby was so excited, because it was his second sale of the day. He said, "Let me ask you a question. What really made you change your mind? Because I thought I had lost you two for good."

They looked at each other and said, "Carlos."

Bobby said, "Who is Carlos?"

Then the man said, "Doesn't Carlos work for you?"

"No," he said.

The receptionist paged Bobby to the showroom. When he thought about it, he came to realize that this was Carlos, the guy who sold the couple the car. Bobby pulled him to the side and asked him, "Why are you working at that fast food restaurant?"

Carlos said, "I need a job to pay bills."

Bobby said, "I saw what you did with that couple back there. Why don't you just work with us?"

Carlos thought about it and consulted with his wife that night. He told her, "You know I love cars. This is a move I need to do for us."

So Carlos was filled with so much love, happiness, motivation, and so much ambition that he could not wait to start. The one thing was, he started off not selling any cars for two months. Bills started to pile up and he was getting frustrated and disappointed because he knew this was what he loved doing, anything that pertains to cars. But all his hard work did not pay off yet. Everyone would tell him don't worry, you will make a lot of sales very soon, just be patient. He realized that in the car business, one of the most important things is to be very patient. So a couple more weeks passed and then one day, a couple walked into the dealership, looking for a car. Carlos asked them, "Can I help you?"

The couple said, "Yes, we are looking for a family-size car."

So he found a car for them and they test-drove it and sat at his desk. The couple did not come to terms with each other to show how they both felt about the car. Well, Carlos had in his mind that they were going to say no already, but he never gave up. So Carlos picked up an application to fill out with the couple and they said, "Yes, we will get the car."

He said, very shocked, "You will?"

They repeated it again, "Yes, we will."

Carlos was so filled with joy, he went into the bathroom, dropped down to one knee and said, "I did it." While he was saying that, a tear started to roll down his face. He was not crying because he was upset, nor was he crying because he had to fill out the whole application. He cried because he was patient, plus he was patient with something he enjoyed in life.

After that day, that was it. The next month he had made the most car sales in the office. The month after that he had gotten second most in the region. A year later he had the most car sales in the whole state of California. This is what having patience in life can do.

I know of a lot of people who give up on the things they truly love and enjoy. They then replace it with something quickly that they hate. You have to be patient, there is no way around it. No one, and I mean no one in life ever made it without having patience. The road is always tough for anyone famous that you may know. It was never easy and it will never get easier.

I want you to think for a second of all the people you know who made it in life and they were not patient. I am not talking about the ones who said they were going to give up and did not, because a lot of people who made it have said the same thing as well. Now think of all the people who have given up on their dream, or they have stopped seeing their vision or put their plan away. You know what happens to these people; they start living in the past. Everything they say and do becomes the past. They tell everyone, "I remember that I was doing that at one time but it got hard." Or else, "I wish I would have opened up that store or gone back to school." You may know some people like that.

Just think of your favorite athlete, entertainer or anyone else you may know who is rich. Do you think the status they have now, they got because they were not patient? No, each and every person was patient, regardless of age, weight, height or race. They must have been patient to get there. It did not come overnight for anyone. Did you also know that 60% of rich people did not reach their success till they became at least the age of 47? Think about the people who have been following their dream since they were 21. That is over 25 years of being patient. So whatever you want to do, just remember you must be patient. You can make it. You can be rich.

BEING TOO COMFORTABLE WITH WHERE YOU ARE IN LIFE

Most rich people never ever get too comfortable. They never just settle for whatever it is in life they have. Let's take movie stars, for example. Some movie stars get two million dollars to five million dollars to 10 million dollars; some even get 20 million dollars. Yes, 20 million dollars just to do one movie.

Here is a list of stars who get close to or at least 20 million dollars. You tell me how many of these actors you have only seen in just one movie.

Bruce Willis   Denzel Washington

Tom Hanks   Will Smith

Nicolas Cage   Julia Roberts

Robert DeNiro

Think for a second: if you made a million dollars, what is the first thing you would do? Quit your job? There is a good chance that's all you may do. Do you know why? Because you would feel comfortable. Well, if you're not a millionaire, how come you are not trying your hardest right now? Because you are comfortable. You should never get too comfortable in life. For those of you who are fooling yourselves, saying everything is fine when you know it is not, whether it be your relationship with someone, your job or it can be your life: Don't make it seem like everything is fine when it is not.

Everything should be fine, but you know that it is not. In relationships when people settle down, get engaged, or get married they tend to get too comfortable with their mate. Some may start off sending roses, cooking dinner, writing poems, washing clothes or just making time for that person. Well, now you feel just because you and this person have moved in together, gotten married, that you can do whatever you want now. But that is wrong. This person should always feel like they are number 1, no matter what happens. Or it could be your job. You say, "They can't fire me, I am too valuable for them to do anything with me, they need me," and these are some of the things that people say. Not saying anything about your place of life, but if you are not getting promoted or you are not a VP or some type of manager, don't fool yourself. You can be replaced just as fast as you got hired. So don't think the world of yourself, 'cause guess what? There is always someone better than you, no matter how you see it. There is always someone who can do your job better than you. There is someone who can treat your mate better than you.

Responsibility is also another issue a lot of people have when it comes to being comfortable. "Well, I don't want anyone to complain when stuff hits the fan. I don't want people to come to me and say anything. I just don't want anything to go wrong." Well, name some people who *want* something to go wrong. No one does. You will never hear someone say, "I hope everything does not work out." For sure there is no guarantee that everything is going to work out. But there is no guarantee everything is going to go wrong either. How many rich and famous people are there with no responsibility? Everyone you can think of in life had some type of responsibility, so if you plan on making it in life without some type of responsibility, that would be almost impossible.

RICH PEOPLE CHANGE
WHAT THEY CAN AND ACCEPT THE
THINGS THEY CAN'T CHANGE

It is true almost everyone in this world complains about something. The main difference is what everyone complains about. This was written in the Serenity Prayer. It was stated, "Lord, grant me the strength to change things I can, the serenity to accept the things I cannot, and wisdom to know the difference." What an incredibly powerful message. Can you imagine how smoothly your life would run if you really used this message every day of your life?

It is true indeed that rich people may complain. However, their complaints come about things they will try to change, not about the things they have no control over.

In every business there are things we must deal with. There are things we can change, that we have some power to control. There are other things that are absolutely beyond our control. Yet how often do we spend our time doing absolutely nothing about the things we do have control over, while whining and complaining about the things we can't do anything about?

One of the main reasons for this is only because we have our priorities twisted in the wrong direction. So once we get our focus right, accept what we have to change and the things that we can, we will have our minds in proper perspective and focus only on those things that we have some capacity to control. It's easy to get back on track.

A friend named Michele, wanted to open her own hair salon. She went to school to learn how to become a beautician. She graduated with flying colors. She worked in a hair shop for about two years. She felt it was time to open her own shop. She was told there were a few things she would have to do in order to open up a shop. Some of the things were get a business plan, find a very good location, open up a bank account, try to save up as much money as she could. She was told another step she should think about taking was getting an investor's loan from the bank. She had a business plan put together. She searched and searched till she found a very good location. She applied for an investor's loan at the same time she opened up a bank account. It took a few weeks but she was approved for the loan. The only problem was the building she was purchasing was residential, which means it was property that was used before to live in, but she wanted to use it for commercial. Commercial is property you use for business, which means she had to get it converted to commercial, which would have to include getting an attorney involved with the building. So she complained that she did not think she should have to do all this extra running around just to switch the building from residential to commercial.

There was no sense for her to complain, because in this case there was nothing she could do about it. She complained so much she backed out of the deal. Someone else bought the property and switched it over to commercial and opened a hair salon and made out very well. Now Michele found a place, not as good as the first one, but it is all right.

Had Michele never complained, she would have been okay. If she would have accepted what she could not change, she would have done well for herself.

There are always going to be things you are going to have to except. Being second is something everyone has to except in life. You and only you will know when it is time to become #1.

Remember in life no matter what you do, you always should strive for the best, but being second is not so bad, especially if you work harder to become #1. But being second is something that can and will change in life. If you want to go out and make changes in your life to be better why not change a few things in life to help you become better.

One of the main things you must do is be willing and ready to take risks. This is another main area that rich people do, to take risks.

Last but not least you must, I repeat, you must surround yourself with people who are trying to do what it is you are trying to do, or with positive people. This is very important. Hang around people who want to change or want more in life than the people you already know who don't.

RICH PEOPLE ARE CRAZY AND MOST EVERYONE ELSE IS INSANE

Everyone who is rich and famous, I am sure they have been called crazy before. The reason they still reach their level of success of becoming rich, even though people have already told them they cannot do it, is because the words that were said to them motivated them even more than they already were. You cannot allow someone to talk you out of your dream. If you do allow someone to talk you out of your dreams, they basically can talk you in and out of any and everything. You can also say they can think for you because that is exactly what they are doing.

One of the reasons these people may talk you out of your dreams is only because they are so afraid to live their own. Don't let anyone choose your life for you. I am sure rich people got told all the time they could not do it. But that did not stop them, so why should you let what they say and feel stop you? These people will stop at nothing to make sure you remember all your downfalls in life and what might happen to you. They never say, "You can do it! I wish you the best! Don't worry, you will not fail if you try that." These people want to see you fail in life, that is what they want. They are afraid you can change to be a better person than they are. Some may not want you to fail but are afraid you may not be as good as you plan on being.

Or else they may have failed before and don't want you to go through that hurting feeling in your life, the same way they may have. You will never know until you try. I don't know if you realized it yet, but the people who may want you to fail or don't want you to follow your dreams for whatever reason, are the same people you may see almost every day, or you might see them 4–5 times a week. I know it sounds bad that the people you know the best would act this way towards you, but that is just the way it is. These are your family members, your co-workers, friends, girlfriends, boyfriends and anyone else you might be close to. These people have the nerve to call you crazy. Don't allow the people to get to you or to change your mind. That is exactly what they want you to do. But don't worry about that. I would rather be called crazy than to live life being insane. That is exactly what these people are—insane.

Let me explain a little about being insane. Insane is when you continue to be somewhere you don't like being, you feel stuck, but you stay. You don't know why you are there, and you are just hoping and waiting for something to just happen. Insane is knowing something is bad or not right for you, but you choose to stay there anyway. Insane is knowing your talents in life, but you always find excuses for why you can't follow your dreams. That is what the world is filled with, people whom I consider to be insane.

You know what I also consider insane? When someone works for over 35–40 years at one place, waits to retire and tells themselves and their spouse, "Now I want to live." You want to wait till you are about 65 years old to really live and have fun? That is insane. No disrespect to anyone that may be reading this and this is your plan, but you have been living for over 50 years. You should have done a lot of things already. You should not wait till this part of your life to live. You should have been living years ago.

If you know someone with a dead-end job who hates what it is they are doing, they are staying there just because they have to pay bills and they are hoping one day everything will change, I consider them insane. Insane people often tend to call others crazy because crazy people are not afraid to live. They are willing to take risks. You can be thought of as being insane if you keep saying, "I am going to wait on this and that," and you really feel that the right time is going to come to you to do whatever it is you want to do.

The only right time is right now. Forget next month, before your check comes or by the time you get the money from your friend or family member. Forget wanting to wait for the second or third semester to sign up for that class you should have taken a while ago. If you think that all these things you want to do are going to chase you for the rest of your life, then you are insane.

If your plan is to make it in life, you must accept certain things in life. One of the things you must accept if you're going to make it, some of your friends and family, co-workers or other people are going to become jealous of you anyway. As you grow, you will come across people who are moving ahead in life, trying to do some of the same things you are trying to do. No one wants anyone to be jealous of them, but you cannot control the way people act towards you. You just have to give everything in life your all. Just try to be yourself. If they don't like you for that, then fine.

Letting go of disapproval is very important. You have to decide what is most important to you. If your main concern in life is to live for other people and to always worry about what everyone else thinks about you, then go ahead and live for everyone else. But let me warn you: you will end up unhappy when you find out later on in life that it is the wrong way to live, unless you don't want anything in life. I know you don't want to live that way. Everything in your life will be considered negative. Every thought that enters your mind and everything you see will be negative. I want you to not forget when you tried to get these same people to see things your way they would never listen to you. So why should you live for them. They are not worried about what you think of them. So don't live according to the way people want you to live or the way they say things will turn out, because you will end up living a life of unhappiness.

I know a girl named Donna. Donna was told at around nine years old she should go to school to be a doctor. She was told that so much that she thought that there was no other way to live her life. As she became a senior in high school her parents spoke so highly of her, she was about to graduate and she would go to college and then to medical school. The main problem was that she was doing it for her parents and not for herself. So of course she graduated college and started in medical school. The only problem was she started to feel medical school and becoming a doctor was not for her. The way she felt about medicine and hospitals started to bother her. She called her parents a few times to tell them that she does not want to be a doctor any longer. They could not understand why. So of course they talked Donna into staying in medical school. She graduated very unhappy about the way her life was going. I don't know many people who graduated from medical school very unhappy, but Donna was.

Now, young Donna was 29, just starting out as a doctor. She had a high-paying job, but was very unhappy about life, frustrated with the job as a doctor. Till one day that all changed. She was on her lunch break, noticed a flyer about taking some computer courses that were given at the local college. She always had a love for computers. The class she was going to take was computer engineering. So she signed up for some courses in computer engineering (which she did love working on computers). She then registered for the classes, and started going to school at night. Two years went by and she was a computer electronic technician and loved it.

The message of this story is enormously important: some of our best success is our life comes at a point where you can't do or live the way you once lived, when you know it is time you stand up and do something you needed to do some time ago. Sometimes as a child growing up you just want to make your family proud of you. What you have to realize is whatever it's in life you want to do and you do it that is fine. You must know as long as you are happy your family should be happy. If you reach a high level of success. They (your family and friends) will be proud of you any way. So in other words if you follow your goals you will not disappoint them any way.

I want you to sit back a second and think about why you ended up in the field you are in now. Was it something you really wanted to do? Was it because someone else wanted you to do it? Or was it because you just needed a job to pay bills? Do whatever it is that pleases you, don't ever do something because you feel you have no choice. There is always a way around things in this lifetime.

FAILURE

No risk to people means no failure. It is very true that failure is an unpleasant feeling. Yes, it is also true that it leaves a nasty taste in your mouth. Yes, it is true that rich people failed 100% more than most people. But you missed one thing: they are rich. Everyone goes through life with some type of failure. It could have been the first time you asked someone out and they said no. It could be the time you did not make the team. Regardless of what had happened in the past, it is over now.

There are only two ways to deal with it: either you learn from it or you run from it. Those are the only solutions I came up with in dealing with failure. You are not just judged on what you do, you are also judged on what you don't do. If you don't do anything, well, that is why you will have nothing. If your fear of failure is what is stopping you, that means you will live the rest of your life not doing something you always wanted to do. When you do that, I hope you know you are just limiting yourself more and more. It is important to remind yourself that most rich people have had many failures in their lives. The difference is that rich people pick themselves up and go on to the next successful thing. You might think that is easier said than done. It is only as hard as you make it. Failure can be the best thing that can happen to you.

Let's say you opened your own store. Business starts off doing real well, but after a while you notice things starting to die down. From that point on, you know if you don't do something quick, you may lose your business. There is a chance you may have to sell the store and all the equipment in the store. So maybe you found out that owning a store was not all it was cracked up to be. Let me ask you this: did you fail? No, you did not fail, you tried your hardest. You got the store, it just did not work out the way you wanted it to work out. That is all, but you are not a failure by far. I am for sure if you opened up another store somewhere else, you'd know what to do to be successful.

See, some people look at failure when they try their hardest, but don't have the results they wanted. Failure comes when you don't try at all. Failure comes when you fail to try, that is failure. Or once you decide to give up, throw in the towel, that is failure.

There also can be a flip side to failing. Failure is something good because it opens other doors to opportunity. Failure is a good thing because it is written in pencil. Not a marker or a pen, but a pencil. The reason it is written in pencil is because it can be erased.

Back a while ago people thought of Thomas Edison as a fool. Thomas Edison was nowhere near a fool. He became a telegrapher before the age of twenty. He became known as the greatest inventor of all time. There was a point where people did not take him serious. But he did not care. People would say to him, "How can you live with yourself? You tried several different things over and over, about ten thousand, but you have failed such a great amount of times out of your life. Don't you feel ashamed of yourself? How can you live with yourself?" Thomas sat back and said, "I know ten thousand things that won't work." Thomas was a man who dealt with a few failures in his lifetime, but never let any of that stuff stop him from reaching greater heights.

I am sure you have heard of the basketball player Michael Jordan, who some may consider the greatest player to have ever played the game of basketball. He made up a commercial talking about all his failures as a kid and even in the game of basketball in his pro career. "In my lifetime, I have been cut from basketball in the tenth grade. I lost over 350 basketball games in all of my life. I missed over 57 game-winning shots. I have fouled out over ten games."

I continue to fail, and fail and fail over and over again. That is why I succeed. I hate for this too be harsh, but there are only two ways to look at everything in my sight. Failure is going to do one of two things: either it will make you want more or want less. There is no in between. Here are a few things that there can not be a in between.

Win or Lose

True or False

Real or Fake

Drive or Walk

Friend or Foe

Rich or Poor

Either you know or you don't know.

When it comes to failure, people tend to forget the good stuff and only focus on the bad. I am not saying by far you should forget about the bad things, but you should focus on the good much more often.

I knew a guy named James who was considering on buying a new Chevy Suburban. He already had two friends who both had purchased a Chevy Suburban that James wanted to purchase. His friends' names were Josh and Sam. James wanted to wait a while before he was going to purchase the truck, because he wanted to pay for the truck in full. But in order to do that, he was going to have to wait for at least one year and save up some more money.

Well, a whole year had passed and his friend Josh enjoyed the vehicle very much. He never had any type of problem with the truck. He loved everything about his truck. He was very happy with his new ride. However, his other friend, Sam, had all types of problems with the truck. He explained to James how he had to get new brakes after two months of having the truck. He would always complain about how much money he would spend on gas every week. So like most people, James did not end up getting the truck he always wanted, only because he ended up taking what his friend Sam said into consideration. Not once did he think about how much his friend Josh enjoyed the truck and how much his friend was in love with the truck. He decided not to get the truck only because one of his friends had such a bad experience with the truck.

The moral of this story is, don't let someone else's failure stop you from what you want in life. Just because something does not work out for someone else does not mean that the same thing cannot work out for you. Also, don't just focus on the negative instead of the positive. If you do this the rest of your life, you will miss out on a lot of things.

HAVING FAITH AND
BEING A BELIEVER

All rich people have some type of faith in what it is they are trying to do. It is that feeling they have in knowing everything is going to work out.

For someone to have faith is very important. These are feelings that are built inside of you. Rich people have faith in everything they do. They never talk or think negative at any time. Even if you ever catch them speaking negatively, they will always keep the faith. To have faith is to never give up. You want to be rich, you have to feel rich already. You have to know you are going to be rich.

The visions you have of yourself, start carrying yourself the same way you see yourself in your visions. You want to be a doctor, you have to see yourself as a doctor already. You want to be a lawyer, you have to see yourself as a lawyer. Believe it or not, inside of you rests a small part in your body that already knows you have what it takes to get to the level you want to be at. Where do you think some of their visions came from? The reason I know, because you pictured yourself in that big house, that nice car, having family and friends over in that big beautiful house, having a big barbecue with everyone you know. But having faith can get you there. Faith works hand in hand with having a vision. But we never put this part of our brain to work. We continue to let it rest and it sleeps more and more each day. But it is time to let that alarm clock go off. It is time to keep that part of you keeping the faith.

You must believe it. I say if you can see it, you can be it, but you have to believe it. I want you to have faith. You may think it is not that simple, but it is as simple as you make it. Believe it or not.

If you want to be successful, all you have to do is just start taking your first step. The next one is take your second step, then take your third. The rest will come easy.

Let me make another point to you. Most people who are not successful always say, "I have to wait to be able to do this," or "I got to pay this off." To be honest, these people who make up all these excuses don't succeed.

Don't you know that you can make excuses and you can make money, but you can't do both? The reason why is because people who make excuses for things in life will always try to say they are waiting for things to be in their favor in order to take that next step. If you are one of these people or know someone like that, the question that should be asked is who is kidding who. You know for sure when you want to do something or not. So if you really want something that bad, you would sacrifice for it. But if you are going to keep telling yourself and the world that when the time is right you are going to do it, nobody is going to believe you but yourself. The world will not believe it, so it comes out to be you keep telling yourself that. See, the thing is you have to attempt to take the first step right now. Not next month, not next year. You must take your first step now. If you don't take that first step now, whatever your excuse was before will end up being your excuse forever.

Along with having faith and believing, there comes persistence. Persistence is a combination of faith, believing, desire and action. A few people are willing to try anything once, but as soon as they have their first let-down they give up. They give up at the first sign of opposition or misfortune. Having lack of persistence is one of the major causes of failure.

Say, "I can do it because I believe I can do it."

You see, rich and successful people surround themselves with everything positive. That way negative thoughts do not enter their minds.

BEING A FOLLOWER AND
BEING A LEADER

The definition of being a follower:

Follower: One in service of another. One who follows the opinions or teachings of another. One who imitates another. One who chases, means one who gives full loyalty and support to another.

Being a follower is something that everyone has experienced before in their lifetime. Rich people do it as well. Being a follower is not always a bad thing. As long as you don't start off as a follower and end up as a follower, you will be fine. However, there are some things in life you will receive as a leader that you will never receive if you stay a follower.

Some people start off as followers and stay followers forever. But being a follower or a leader to you are part of a team.

There are also different types of followers in life. You may have the type of person who follows just because that person is scared to be the way they really want to be. For example, if you know someone who is in a gang or always followed the wrong crowd just because that person just wanted to feel like he or she was a part of something. This person could be told to do things. Knowing that it was wrong and knowing they did not want to do it, this person would do it anyway. You have the people who may be assistant supervisor but never get to the level of head supervisor. Not because that person is not good enough; they just don't want to deal with the pressure that the lead person gets.

Another thing about being a follower is you will never receive the rewards that most leaders receive if you always stay second.

The definition of being a leader:

A leader is someone who ranks first. A person who leads as a guide or conductor. A person who directs. One who has commanding authority or influence. One who is placed in advance of a team. A principal performer of a group.

If you never step out to the floor front, you will live a life filled with thinking, "I could do that job, but I am not ready to be a leader." You have to try.

Followers do exactly what they do best: just follow, go with the flow. You must not do that. You have to do what the rich do. They can be a follower, but they know in their mind that will not last long. The reason that will not last long is because they learn how to separate themselves from everything else.

However, everyone cannot lead. There has to be someone to follow. If everyone tries to lead, then you all will fail. If everyone tries to follow, then you all will still fail. This world is not meant to have everyone to be a leader. If you enjoy being second, that is fine. Just don't be a follower of something you know you should not be following. Don't become a follower to people who can't lead at all.

Separate yourself. Rich people have to separate themselves from all of the things in their life. Now, when I say separate I don't mean they (rich people) go sit on top of their roof and not talk to anyone. What I mean is they do not allow other things in their life to distract them from whatever it is they are trying to do in life. If you are trying to focus on life, don't let anything stop you from getting to the next level.

Earvin "Magic" Johnson, the basketball player, separated himself from everything else in the world when he was growing up. He always had friends but he did not play around with them all the time. His friends would come by his house and ask him to play with all the other little kids on the street. Magic would say no, and continue playing basketball by himself. It would not matter if it started raining, snowing or if it began to get dark. He would continue to work hard and separate himself from everything else. He did not want to be like everybody else. He knew what it was he wanted to do. That is why he separated himself. I am sure you can tell it paid off big time for him.

Before I started writing this book, I would play cards all the time. For weeks, that is all I did. I told my friends a while in advance that I was planning on writing a book. Which meant that I was not going to play cards until I was done with my book. Of course they did not believe me. Well, as you can tell, I did put playing cards on hold for a very long time. That is because I knew I had to separate playing cards from writing a book. I felt that writing this book was much more important. I know I like going out sometimes and most people do, but I would have to choose a lot of other things that are much more important to me. See, when you allow other things to enter your life, it begins to push other things more and more to the back of your life. This all comes in at the point when you have to be willing to change.

BE WILLING TO CHANGE

Everyone who is rich and famous had to change something in their life. I don't care if it was not going to church, changing the wardrobe, the schedule, eating habits. Whatever habit that person may have had, they had to change something. The only difference between you and that rich person you may admire is whatever in your life you will not change or will not try to change, I am sure someone rich was more willing to make the change and they did.

Change is as important as anything else you may consider being important. You must want to do things differently so you can get better results out of life. How many things in your life do you know offhand you should change? The question you need to ask yourself is why you have not tried to change. You can't sit here and say you are going to be a person who is going to continue to live your life the way you have been living and be successful. You must make a change. You have to make a change right now. The change must start in you. I know you get tired of that empty feeling you get inside. That feeling comes from you knowing you should be living differently. I know a lot of you are reading this book, saying I am sick and tired of this. I am sick and tired of that. Or else you are saying I am sick and tired of being sick and tired.

Well, I know firsthand that making a change in life is not that easy. But the flip side to it is not that hard either. I know one of the main reasons it may seem hard is only because you are accustomed to doing this. "I have always done it this way" or "I thought about that but I just did not do it." Well, think about this: look at what you have now. Is it everything you always wanted or do you want more out of life? If it is not what you always wanted, then how do you expect things to change in your life, if you don't do things any differently? If you want more, you have to do more.

I want you to sit back and think of all the things you need to change in your life. After you think about it, start writing them down. After you have written them down, choose the main thing that you find hard to change about yourself. Whatever it may be, I want you to go through with the change for just five days and see how it goes. The next thing you should do after the five days is up to yourself. Can you go longer than five days? I am hoping your answer comes out to be yes. If your answer is yes, then you are on your way. Your very next step is to go on with the next hardest thing on the list you need to change. Try this for just as long. See how well you can do with these two things. You may be surprised at yourself if you try. Right after that, go to the third item on your list. But the next thing you should do is go right back to number one. You have to make sure at this point you should be doing all of them at the same time. See, once you begin to make changes in your life, you can start letting things go as well. That comes along with being spiteful, holding grudges or any other negative thing that may have some effect on you looking towards your future.

LETTING IT ALL GO

Most rich people always let things go. They don't have to be spiteful. They don't have to hold on to grudges in their life. Think about when you tell a child to stop playing around. The first thing that they say is he or she started it. Can you be mad at them for that? No, you have absolutely no reason to be mad at them for that. You know why? You do the same thing. The only difference is you are older than the children. It is very immature to be spiteful.

I am no better than you, because I have done it many moons ago. I realize I was too old for that. You can't expect to live life like that. See when you hold grudges or become spiteful towards people you end up finding yourself trying to avoid this one person. Then you have to try to hide from this person. You keep your words very limited. Or you may try to do something to revenge whatever it was done to you. I don't know about you, but I am too old to hide from people just because I don't want that person to see me. You ever thought about if that person is living the way they want to live, so why should you be hiding and thinking of an evil way to tie up the score? But the only thing is there is no game, you are the only one playing it. If that is the case, you should just play with the kids if you are going to be that way. Please, I ask you to stop holding grudges and stop being spiteful. You will burn yourself out like that.

This will help you in the long run. Forget that co-worker, friend, cousin, aunt, uncle, mother, father, sister and brother you are not talking to. Be the bigger person. Stop being spiteful, let it go. "Why should I do that for them? They would never do that for me." Let it go. "I am not going to this place because I know he or she will be there."

Whatever grudge you have against someone, let it go.

I had grudges in the last few years I had to let go. I have a female friend I have been holding a grudge against for about 4–7 years, only because she would hang out with her other male friends and would not go out with me often. I also did not know she just started a second job and also just enrolled to go back to school. Once I realized I was a fool to try to duck her and not speak to her just because I did not get the attention I wanted, I spoke to her about it. The whole time it was a guy who was trying to get with her, she also started to date him. I felt dumb because for all these years I thought she said something that she did not even say. Just to break the whole grudge thing, what I did was write a letter to her saying I don't know if she had any bad feelings built up towards me, but I just wanted to let her know that I loved her. She wrote me back saying she did not have any bad feelings built up towards me. Ever since then I have been more happy.

I had a friend who asked me to get a cell phone put in my name that was going to be on my credit. I said okay, fine. A few months passed and I tried to get a cell phone and the cell phone company told me I was not approved, that I could not get a phone. I was very surprised because I had good credit. I called up AT&T. They told me my bill was $1,000.25. I was so dumbfounded that it honestly took me a while to figure out who had a phone in my name. So I tried to track my friend, but it was too late. There was nothing I could do. That hurt my credit for a few years. So I figured I would not pay the bill. But I realized that I would only hurt myself, so I ended up paying for it. I never did talk to the guy, but if you are reading this book I just want you to know I am not mad at you, but it would be nice to get some money from it. If not, I am going to keep it moving. Hey Jayson, if you are reading this, you don't have to duck me anymore.

Also let me explain what letting go of everything does. It builds character, it helps you to live a better life. Just think of all the times you are told to do extra work that you should not be doing. You never know who is watching you and admiring you. Don't allow small things get to you, let it go. I am not suggesting you let people get over on you, but don't hold on to extra baggage. Just remember when you are asked to do things that can be something extra, you have learned something new again, instead of being something you refused and lose.

Just don't be spiteful. I want you to think about how many spiteful people do you know that are rich, that you know personally? If you don't know, maybe it's because they are always willing to let stuff go. To be honest, holding grudges and being spiteful may block out a lot of stuff as far as you becoming lucky.

BEING LUCKY

Think there is no such thing as luck? There is such a thing as luck. If you were in a car with three of your friends and you all got in a car accident and you were not injured but they were injured, would you consider that luck? Yes. If you read this whole book, follow your goals in life and become successful, is that some type of luck? Yes. Now when I am talking about luck, I am not talking about four-leaf clovers, horseshoes or a rabbit's foot. I am talking about being at the right place at the right time. That is luck within itself. When you find someone, they may be a bad person and you thought they were nice. If you find this out before you get involved with them in any way, I consider you to be very lucky. So start creating your own luck. Start putting yourself in the position to be lucky. Let's forget about the stuff that is not getting us anywhere. Let's be lucky for now and the rest of your life. A lot of people consider rich people to be lucky. But the whole point is you must take risks in order to become lucky. You must try extra, work extra to get extra. You can consider extra to be lucky. So you must try to create your own luck.

BEING CONFUSED

Being confused is something that everyone goes through. It does not matter if you are short, tall, skinny, fat, white, black, rich or poor. However, the only difference is the amount of time you allow yourself to stay confused. Someone rich looks at a situation and then narrows down their options. A lot of times they get insight from others who may have been in the same situation. When they do narrow down their options, they basically write down their choices. They take a sheet of paper, fold it in half. They would write columns A and B. Write down the pros and cons, make their decisions and get on with their life.

When you are feeling confused about some situation, you continue to keep putting it off, no matter what it is. The second thing that most people do is get advice from someone who knows less than they do about the situation. Most of the time you may even listen to them. Why? Who knows why? It can be for numerous reasons, but whatever reason you try to justify in your mind, you should not expect the outcome to be the way you want it to be.

To be honest, to ask someone who knows everything about the situation you are in, is common sense. You don't go to a doctor for legal advice, you go to a lawyer. You don't go to a lawyer for medical advice, you go to the doctor. If you want soda, you don't go to the milkman. So your best bet is to get advice from people who have been where you are trying to go or people who are going through the same situation that you are in.

See, being confused also can help you when you have to make bigger and bigger decisions in the near future. Also, when you don't make a decision on whatever it may be that you are confused about, you are allowing the decision to be made by itself. At that point you have no say until the decision is settled. Know when you are confused, make sure you get your sheet of paper and fold it in half. Write column A and column B. Point out all the good and bad points in each column. After you do this, believe it or not, your answer will become commonsense.

RELATIONSHIPS

For some rich people, there are different situations. There are some who don't get involved until they have already reached certain levels of greatness. There are some who stay single because they are so focused on what they are trying to do. There are so many of them who do not trust another person. The main reason for that is some feel they may be trying to get them for all the things they have worked hard for.

But if this person is married, that means more than likely this person or wife was very supportive to some level. To be honest, as long as you have support, you have faith. As long as you have faith, you win, not lose.

Most people who are dating may have different situations. If you find yourself trying to advance to the next level of your life and you feel the person you are with is not supportive or understanding, that can and will cause a problem. By all means, if you are married, you should never get in a debate with your spouse about putting that person second. However, if you married this person and you two plan on spending the rest of your lives together, that person should not have to wonder if they are #1 in your life.

If you are dating, the situation came out to be a little different. The reason being you and this person are getting to know each other better. So that might bring problems to the new relationship trust you may have. Also some people are very, very selfish. They may not want you to follow your dream. Reason being is because they may feel you following your dream is stopping them from spending time with you. At this time you are put in a position where you have to decide is your dream as important as your relationship is. If you feel you cannot live without both, it is important that you let this person understand what it is that you are doing. Why you are doing it. How they can help you. Believe it or not, this person can help you more than you think.

If you are in a situation where you are involved with someone and you feel it is not going anywhere, plus you feel this person is hurting you more than helping you, there is a reason for you and this person not to be together. Please don't just read this chapter, then go home and start dumping people. That is not the solution. But if you want the person around, then sit down and discuss it over with them. Just do not say that being in that relationship with someone is the reason you can't or will not be rich, because that is not true. There are always ways to work around things.

THERE ARE NO GREAT PEOPLE.
EVERYONE IS HUMAN,
BUT SOME DO GREAT THINGS.

This title is so very true. All the rich, famous people in the world are no better than you, from Mark McGuire to Michael Jordan, from Elton John and Shaquille O'Neal to the Backstreet Boys to Jagged Edge. All these celebrities are not great people. They may perform great at times but are still, normal people. Some may even seem to be perfect. Humans are not perfect. Don't think of these people as being perfect because that is not true.

You may not do a lot of great things, but never ever sell yourself short of who you are. You just have to try a little bit harder at what you are doing. To be honest, the only thing that separates the normal people from everyone else is the titles of the chapters to this book. Writing out a plan, being patient, etc.…

So all these so-called greats can be you. Just eliminate all the negatives that you may have in your life and you can be great. But you must tell yourself that you are great. You must be focused. These people are also people who never quit. Because none of these people are quitters. They will never give up. So if you want to succeed you cannot quit. You have to work hard. The only place where success comes before work is in the dictionary.

THE TRUE MEANING OF
BEING RICH

Having abundant possessions and material wealth. Having high value or quality. Rich implies having more than enough to gratify normal needs or desires.

My last and final topic is the meaning of being rich. Rich, of course, is having everything you may have ever wanted. You may have wanted to take trips to places and go to see a lot of different sights in life. Rich is not necessarily having money. Yes, you can be rich with what you have and what you do. That does not mean you are wealthy, rich with money. If you are doing something you enjoy and love, money will appear on you. To travel to success you have to think of yourself as being rich already.

Just knowing you have a love for what ever it is you want to do in life is being rich. To just vision all the different things you want to do and to one day actual do them is rich. Rich is not always looking in your back account to see how much money you have. Rich is about getting all you ever wanted and knowing you worked hard for it.

This is my first book. The moment I decided I was going to write a book I became an author, and was not considered an author after the book was edited or published. That second I realized I was going to write a book. If your main goal is to become rich with a lot of wealth, you must change to act the way a wealthy person would.

Start doing what rich people do and stop doing what they will not be doing—procrastinating, making excuses, not making changes in your life. Don't worry that it is too late, or "I should have done this a while ago" or "I can't do it right now."

All of these words are lies. Forget "you might" or "you can" because you will. The main thing you have going for you is time. But also remember, time waits for no one. I hope this book helped you to understand the reason why only a few people are rich and a lot people are not. I just want you to realize that you can be what ever you want to be. All you have to do is go after it. What ever excuse and reason you feel is holding you down, should be a reason to motivate you more. I don't care what it is you can come out on top. I promise you. All you have to do is try harder.

If you feel you are working hard now, then try your hardest you will be very surprised with the results. I hope you have learned from it. Whatever it is that is going on in your life you can turn it all around. Just know it in your heart. I know you can be rich. Just determine what ever it is you want and it can be yours.

Here are a few quotes I live by day by day.

If you have money you should give often.

If you don't have enough money you should give away more often.

–T.D. Lowman

In life you don't get what you want.

You get what you are.

–Les Brown

If you believe in God, you should not pray to him about your problems.

You should tell your problems about your God.

–Unknown

The true measure of a man's wealth is in the thing he can afford not to buy.

–Ralph Waldo Emerson

I don't know the key to success, but I do know the key to failure is trying to please everyone else.

–Bill Cosby

The only place where your dream becomes impossible is in your own thinking.

–Robert H. Schuller

There are no great people in this world, only great challenges that ordinary people rise to meet.

–William Frederick Hulsey Jr.

Always look at what you have left.

Never look at what you have lost.

−Robert Schuller

Conditions are never just right. People who delay actions until all factors are in their favor never end up doing anything.

−William Feather

The word can't died in the battle of try.

−Unknown

The failure of one thing is repaired by the success of another.

−Thomas Jefferson

Seek your goals and they will find you.

–Les Brown

It is always better to lose a debate to a wise old man, than to win a debate with a young fool.

–T.D Lowman

If you want the rainbow, you have to put up with the rain.

–Dolly Parton

Fools look to tomorrow: wise men use tonight.

–Scottish proverb

Men talk of killing time, while time quietly kills them.

–Dion Boucicalt

Shoot for the moon. Even if you miss, you will land among the stars.

–Les Brown

As long as you are going to be thinking anyway, think big!

–Donald Trump

You are never given a dream without also being given the power of making it come true.

–Richard Bach

All forms of fear produce fatigue.

–Bertrand Russell

Fear makes strangers of people who should be friends.

–Shirley Maclaine

It is very hard to fail, but it is worse never to have tried to succeed.

–Theodore Roosevelt

It is easy to live life hard, but it is hard to live life easy.

–T.D Lowman

T. D. Lowman

ABOUT THE AUTHOR

I remember growing up in my younger days. I lived my life trying to be like everyone else. I always tried to fit in with everyone. You may still be living like this now or know someone who may be living this way now. I guess you can say I was programmed to be that way. All I ever heard was go to school, find a job, work for about 25–40 years at some company and then retire. So when you retire you can just live off of your 401k. All my friends were doing what their parents wanted them to do. I did the same thing as well but when I thought about it, I would end up living an unhappy life that way.

I still remember when I graduated from high school, working at McDonald's, my father would tell me, "You should go to school for computers. In this field you can make a lot of money and this is the wave of the future, so just find a computer school to go to. This is what you should do with your life." Just like anyone else, I always wanted to make my parents proud of me. I remember our family had a cookout and we had a few family members over. Well, that day I went to the park to play basketball. When I came back, I walked through the door and I overheard my father telling my uncle that I would do well in the computer field and this would be the best thing for me. He also said that he was proud that I was going this direction. So I felt like I had to get involved with computers. I could not let my father down.

So I went to this computer school and took up computer programming. The course was for only 10 months. I ended up graduating with a 3.4 grade point average. I learned a lot about computers, but I was not happy. I knew this was not what I wanted to do with the rest of my life. I had a lot of job offers making $35,000 a year, but I did not take any of the great job offers I was getting. I was going to be 19, making close to $40,000 a year, and that would have been great. I did not pursue it because it was not the job for me. After that I kept trying to find temp jobs. I would go from job to job, just working for a few days or a few weeks for $6 here or $7 there.

So I went from job to job, looking for employment. I knew the only reason why I did not take the computer job was because I knew I would have felt stuck. I did not even like computers after a while because he would brag about me going to this school. How many of you ever felt this way before or know someone who may feel this way now?

Well, I found all different types of jobs until I got into real estate. I found something I enjoyed. Within the last two years this has been the thing for me. When you find something you like, you normally find something else that you may enjoy as well. Like for me, I found myself wanting to help people more and more. So while doing the real estate, I found my next true love. I want my next move to become a motivational speaker. I am just here to say I hope you enjoy my book and I don't care what your dream is, but don't sell yourself short. If you work hard at whatever it is you want to do, go ahead and do it. Forget what everyone else may say. If you don't have anyone in your corner, I will be in your corner.

Rich people don't ever sell themselves short. So why should you sell yourself short? I just want to thank you for reading my book. Look for my next book, "Are You Tired Yet?" coming out in the summer of 2002.

There are great things put here for you and me to have in this lifetime. We must take advantage of everything that is given to us. If you are a person who wants more in life, who doesn't want to live from check to check, and who does care how your future may end up, then this is the perfect book to make your bookshelf look nicer.

If you are a person who wants to change the way things are, wants more out of life, don't want to hold back any longer, tired of getting treated like you are nothing, then this book is for you.

If you want to find out why people become successful, this is the right book. If you have some ambitions and desires, you want to bring them to fulfillment and you want to be well off, this is the way to go—read this book:

THE REASONS WHY THEY'RE RICH AND YOU'RE NOT.

Printed in the United States
2758

9 780759 655065